10 WALKS UNDER 6 MILES

Dalesman

First published in 2005 by Dalesman
an imprint of
Country Publications Ltd
The Water Mill
Broughton Hall
Skipton
North Yorkshire BD23 3AG

First Edition 2005
Updated edition 2013

Text © Mary Welsh 2005
Maps © Gelder Design & Mapping 2005
Illustrations © Christine Isherwood 2005

Cover: Ullswater from Arthur's Pike by Tom Parker

A British Library Cataloguing-in-Publication record
is available for this book

ISBN 978-1-85568-218-4

Printed by 1010 Printing International Ltd

PUBLISHER'S NOTE
....
The information given in this book has been provided in good faith and is intended only
as a general guide. Whilst all reasonable efforts have been made to ensure that details
were correct at the time of publication, the author and Country Publications Ltd
cannot accept any responsibility for inaccuracies. It is the responsibility of individuals
undertaking outdoor activities to approach the activity with caution and, especially if
inexperienced, to do so under appropriate supervision. The activity described in this book
is strenuous and individuals should ensure that they are suitably fit before embarking
upon it. They should carry the appropriate equipment and maps, be properly clothed and
have adequate footwear. They should also take note of weather conditions and forecasts,
and leave notice of their intended route and estimated time of return.

Contents

Introduction

These ten fine circular walks — six miles long or less, and all at under 1,500 feet — start from the shores of Ullswater, a beautiful and completely unspoiled lake. It is believed to be named after L'Ulf, a Norse settler. It is a long, winding lake scooped out by a retreating glacier during the last Ice Age. The rock strata beneath the lake differed in hardness, and so resisted the glacier to different degrees. As a result, the lake has two pronounced bends, giving it a serpentine shape. Because of the lake's bends, Donald Campbell, who made many trial runs on the lake in his attempt on the world's water speed record, found it unsuitable for his final fatal run, which he made on Coniston Water.

Becks rising high in the spectacular surrounding fells flow fast into the lake from many stunning side valleys, through which several of these walks take you. The lake's water flows into the River Eamont at Pooley Bridge, from where three walks start. The land around the foot of Ullswater, flatter than all the other land about the lake, is composed of sandstone and limestone, resulting in glorious displays of wild flowers during the summer months. The land about the middle reach, composed of softer Skiddaw Slate, is a tranquil tree-clad area with angular hills and grassy tops. Land at the head of the lake is composed of Borrowdale Volcanics, and here are magnificent dramatic fells viewed from several of the walks.

The lake is seven and a half miles long and half a mile at its widest point. Near Stybarrow Dodd at Glencoyne the lake is nearly 200 feet deep. A road runs close to the south-eastern shoreline, where there are lay-bys, shadowed by deciduous trees, and people can picnic, the water is shallow and laps gently on little pebbly beaches. On the opposite shore, a narrow road runs from Pooley Bridge to Howtown which lies about halfway along. The road then moves into side valleys and ends. Near Howtown, below Hallin Fell, fishermen used to stretch a net across this the narrowest part of the lake to catch a whitefish, the schelly, often called a freshwater herring.

On all these walks, Ullswater dominates the scene. So put your boots on, pack your waterproofs and enjoy all that the lake has to offer.

For information on public transport in the area, telephone Traveline on 0871 2002233 or visit www.travelinenortheast.info.

Grisedale

Length of walk: 5¹⁄₂ miles
Time: 3 hours
Terrain: Good tracks and paths, suitable for all the family
Start/finish: Car park on the north side of the A592, opposite the Patterdale Hotel, grid ref 396159
Toilets: Passed early on the walk
Map: OS Explorer OL5

This circular walk from Patterdale car park goes over pastures and along a glorious airy track. After crossing the Grisedale Beck by a footbridge, the walker returns along a good track and a minor road. The views are stunning in their grandeur.

Join the main road by a purpose-built wall gap, from the middle of the rough car park. Cross, with care, and walk left. At the end of the shops, wind right and continue up a track, passing the toilets on the left. Follow the track round right and then take the footpath, left, as signposted. Carry on through a pleasing copse to reach a wider track. Turn left and go through a gate onto the fell. Follow the track for a short distance and, at the wall corner, take the step stile over the wall. The stile is hidden by a tree and is signposted on the far side.

Walk on left from the stile and follow the clearly arrowed way over the pleasing park-like pastures as it descends to a gate onto a track. Turn right

The head of Ullswater.

5

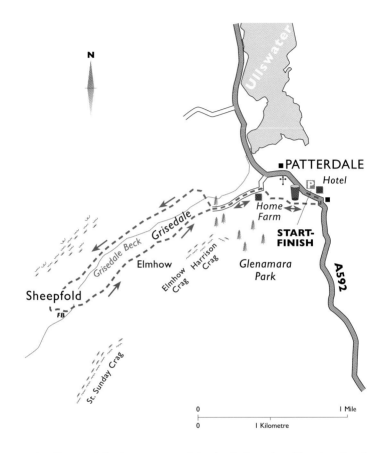

and walk on to join the narrow road that leads from the village into lovely Grisedale. Turn left. Peep over the wall to see the Grisedale Beck hurrying, white-topped, through its very deep wooded gill. Climb the hill and, just before the first gate over the road, turn right along a minor lane. Where it turns right, take the gate ahead and climb the steepish grassy slope. Pause as you go to enjoy the view into the dale while getting your breath back. Go through a gate in the wall and walk a few steps to reach a four-armed signpost.

Turn left, following the direction for Grisedale. Stroll along this pleasing, airy, terrace-like path, high above the beck, as it continues into the dale. Dawdle on to pass through an iron gate in a fence. The pleasing grassy way

Grey wagtails are often seen alongside fast-flowing water such as Grisedale Beck.

continues, with most of the little streams racing down the fell slopes to join the main beck carefully culverted under the path. Carry on along the path, soon to go through another iron gate, with Scots pine on a hillock below to your left. Now you are leaving the more cultivated part of the valley behind. To your left, across the vale, you can see Birks and St Sunday Crag. Ahead, the mountains begin to close in on the head of the valley.

On reaching a ruined shepherd's hut, turn left just before a wooden gate. Descend by the wall, and then follow a green trod, rather indistinct at times, down the fell slope, and continue where it bears left round a hillock. Carry on to a gate in a wall, which gives access to a footbridge over the Grisedale Beck, with St Sunday Crag now towering overhead. Beyond, take a few steps ahead, then follow a narrow path that drifts half left to join a wide track.

Carry on, left, on the stony path. As you go, look across the valley towards your outward route to see the magnificent wall that snakes uphill from your outward path towards broken crags and Striding Edge. Dawdle on through the valley to pass, on your left, a large planting of sycamores. Go on to walk to the right of Elmhow Barn and then pass Elmhow farmhouse, on your right. Just beyond the dwelling, a tumbling waterfall descends through conifers. A few steps on along the track, move over a grassy area, on your left, to see charming Elmhow Bridge, a traditional stone-built arched bridge over the beck.

Walk on along the track, enjoying all that Grisedale has to offer and come, eventually, to the last gate. Beyond, ignore the left turn taken earlier. From here, either continue down the road to Patterdale and turn right, or retrace your steps over the fell slope to arrive at the far end of the village, where you turn left.

Lanty's Tarn

> **Length of walk: 5 miles**
> **Time: 2-3 hours**
> **Terrain: Suitable for all the family including energetic grannies and well-behaved dogs**
> **Start/finish: Glenridding car park in centre of village, grid ref 386170. Bus stop close by.**
> **Toilets in car park.**
> **Map: OS Explorer OL5**

A circular walk from Glenridding car park, along good tracks, through fine deciduous woodland, across open fell on a distinct path, and alongside a tumbling beck.

From the car park at Glenridding, head for the main road and go right. Cross the bridge over Glenridding Beck and turn right again in front of a row of interesting shops. At the signposted Y-junction, take the left branch. Opposite a cottage named Glenkeld, take a short waymarked path going left off the main track.

Pass through a gate and admire the fine waterfall ahead. Bear right. At the next waymark, join the pitched path, which winds left and then right as it ascends steadily through fine deciduous woodland. Sit on the seat on the left of the path, from where you can enjoy your first good view of Ullswater. Then carry on to go through a gate to walk right on a level path, with a fine view of Sheffield Pike ahead.

Ignore the gate ahead and wind sharp left, with another spectacular view ahead. Carry on the pitched way as it levels and comes to a gate. Do not pass through — yet — but turn left to climb a stile. Step across the outflow of the tarn and climb up the green path to a charming grassy flat area on a hillock, Keldas, just made for a picnic. The view through the pines of the lake is superb.

Return downhill to the gate previously ignored and go through to walk beside the pretty tree-girt Lanty's Tarn. It once provided ice for Patterdale

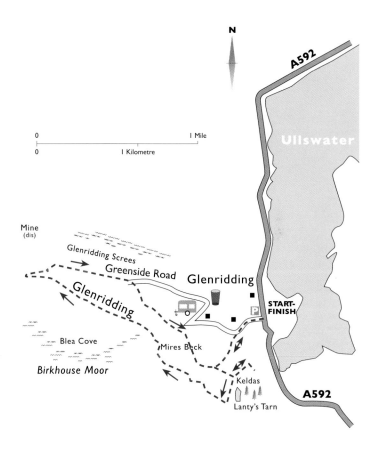

Hall; the bottom of the tarn was cleared of weeds in the summer, and in the winter blocks of ice were cut.

Opposite the small dam, at the end of the tarn, take a narrow path, right, over the fell. Where the path goes sharp left, carry on ahead on a rising path to a stile on the skyline. Beyond, walk on the clear path across the fell slopes, gradually descending to cross a beck. Go on along the distinct way, to come beside a sturdy wall, on your right. Stroll on until the wall turns right, down to the valley. Here go on ahead along a pitched way, which descends to stepping stones across Mires Beck. Beyond, stride the path to descend slightly right, to come beside another friendly wall. Ignore the ladder-stile,

Wood sorrel flowers in April and June.

on your right, and walk along the track beside the continuing wall, still to your right.

Ignore two grassy trods, on the left, ascending the fell, and remain by the wall. Walk on along the airy, terraced path and soon, after you've spotted the weir on the beck below, leave the main track and descend, right, to cross the iron bridge, spanning the beck.

Walk right to pass through the remaining buildings of the old leadmine buildings, now put to other uses. The mine closed in 1962 after being in operation since the eighteenth century. At one time it was the largest leadmine in England, producing massive amounts of lead — and a steady flow of silver for the Bank of England. After closure many of the buildings were removed.

When, in 1927, the mine's dam in Keppel Cove — to your left and high up above this walk — burst, water raced down the valley and swept into the basement of a hotel near the shore, where the maids were sleeping. Fortunately the windows burst before their beds reached the ceiling.

Continue down the track towards Glenridding. After less than half a mile, look for where the wall on the right winds a little right before it continues on. Here, go through an easy-to-miss waymarked gate on the right to follow a grassy trod, half left, down the fell to cross the bridge over the beck once more. Wind round left and walk on along the clear track over a pasture to a gate onto a minor road. Turn left and descend. Just before the road bridge over the beck, turn right to walk a good track beside the river. Follow this delightful way as it climbs a little and then head on along your outward route to return to Glenridding.

Glendridding Dodd

Length of walk: 4 miles
Time: 2-3 hours
Terrain: Steep climb over a stony path to start and then a grassy way as it ascends over the col. Narrow grassy paths from then on. Good track for most of the way through the lower part of the wood. Distinct easy path along the side of the lake.
Start/finish: Glenridding car park, grid ref 386170
Toilets: In car park
Map: OS Explorer OL5

A circular walk from Glenridding car park, climbing steeply at first, and then more easily to the cairn on the heathery summit of Glenridding Dodd (1,425 feet). After following the long wall over the top of the handsome fell, the walker descends beside fine Glencoyne Wood and then through the beeches along Glencoynedale to return beside the lake.

Leave the car park by the top right corner and continue along the road through the houses. Follow it as it winds right and then left. Cross the cattle grid and immediately turn acute right to walk a grassy swathe for a few steps and then sharp left along a grassy terrace. Just before the row of houses, on the left, leave the trod and begin to climb the fell, right, just before a clump of gorse. Go on climbing a very stony track which, though still steep, improves steadily.

Follow the way where it winds left and then goes on up as a wide track, sometimes stony and sometimes grassy, through the bracken, to reach the grassy col. Walk ahead over grass to a gate in the cross wall. Do not pass through the gate but walk right and then wind round left, on a good path, parallel with the wall on your left. Cross a small area of scree on a good path and follow the way to where it turns sharp right and becomes two paths. Take either — they soon join — and stroll on as the pleasing way winds round a hillock. Carry on through a dip and then over another small hump, and ascend gently to the fine cairn on the Dodd. The view of the lake and the fells is superb.

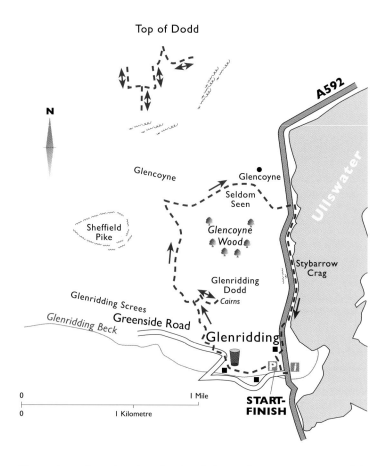

Return down the path to the col and again ignore the gate, now on your right, and walk on along the wall to go right through a purpose-built gap in it. Walk on for a few steps and then follow the path as it begins to climb away from the wall, through the bracken, making a large arc to avoid an area of large boulders by the wall. The rising path then returns to the side of the wall at the brow. To your left tower the rough slopes of Sheffield Pike.

Walk on parallel with the wall on a narrow level path until you come to a row of stately Scots pines, on your right, beyond the wall. From now on, the narrow grassy path descends steadily, distinctly and quite steeply down beside the walled Glencoyne Wood. At the bottom of the longish slope, go

12

The red squirrel favours the quieter areas of Lakes woodland.

over the rickety stile on your right. Stroll on along the pleasing path, just inside the glorious deciduous woodland, to come close, on your left, to a row of cottages — with eleven chimneys — named Seldom Seen. They were built in this lonely spot for the Greenside miners, well away from Glenridding, to discourage them from making use of the pubs in the village.

From here, a good track continues through the fine woodland to the main road. Watch out for red squirrels as you go and look down into the valley, on your left, to see Glencoyne, a traditional, Lakeland farmhouse, with white-washed, rough-cast exterior. Cross the A-road and walk right along the path just beyond the low wall, with the lake to your left. Wind round charming Mossdale Bay and carry on to where you must join the road for a very short distance, below Stybarrow Crag. Here Ullswater is at its deepest.

Then turn left into the woodland again to stroll the idyllic path through the lovely beeches, just above the lapping water, to reach the road once more. Cross and walk on along the pavement for a short distance to return to the car park.

Aira Force

Length of walk: 5¹/₂ miles
Time: 3 hours
Terrain: Suitable for all fit walkers. Children should be under close control at two points on the return walk.
Start/finish: National Trust Aira Force car park, grid ref 401201, on A592, 2¹/₂ miles north-west of Glenridding. Bus stop at car park.
Toilets: In car park
Map: OS Explorer OL 5

A circular walk from Aira Force car park, along good tracks, past two magnificent waterfalls, up a steepish fell path to Gowbarrow's summit, returning along a distinct path high above the shores of Ullswater.

From the back of the car park, follow the good track into deciduous woodland. Go through a gate and then a wall gap into an open area. Head on to take the easily missed steps through a gap on your right, to descend to a footbridge over Aira Beck. Climb the steps beyond. Follow the pitched path, left, passing some exotic trees, including Chilean pine and Douglas firs and many rhododendrons, planted in Victorian times. Where the way divides, take the left branch. Descend gently to cross a footbridge. Look up to see the astounding Aira Force plummeting downwards and roaring noisily against the confining rock-faces.

Return across the bridge and climb the long flight of stone steps, now on your left. Then walk left to stand on the footbridge over the ravine, through which the imprisoned water rages. Ascend more steps to take the track on your right to walk upstream of the Aira. Ignore, but notice, the next footbridge and walk on a rather rougher path. After heavy rain you will spot a wall of white water through the pleasing woodland — your first glimpse of High Force, a glorious 'companion' to Aira Force.

Walk back to cross the footbridge over a narrow deep canyon, noted earlier. Turn left, climb a slope and join a track, heading upstream. Go past the other side of High Force (not seen at its best from here). Follow the track to a wall and then go through a gate, slightly right, into woodland. Where the trees cease, step out onto a rising path into delightful open rolling countryside.

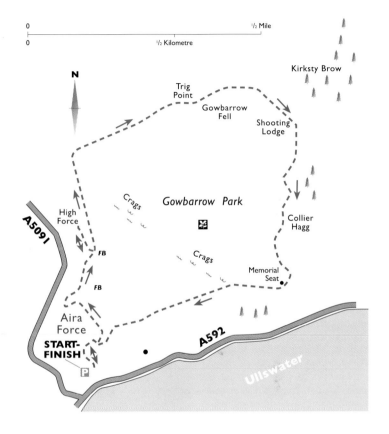

Just before the next gate in the wall ahead, turn right to walk a short permissive path to climb a ladder-stile over the fell wall. Go up the wide, heavily reinforced path beside the walled plantation on your left and, once beyond it, continue on up. Finally a path bears away from the wall and heads up to the trig point on the summit, about which grows heather and bilberries. You will want to pause here to enjoy the magnificent views.

Go straight on from the top, on a clear path, keeping parallel with the continuing wall, away to your left. Carry on downhill and, as the path nears a wall corner, follow the path as it begins to wind right, with a stream and a wall now to your left. Stroll on until you reach a ruin, an old shooting lodge. Here join a wider path and turn right to climb above a steep slope, dropping

15

towards the shore of the lake — a little white-knuckle stretch where children should be under control. Cross the footbridge over Collierhagg Beck. Go on and, where the path divides, take the left branch and continue on the high-level path to wind round a rocky corner.

Stroll on, with care, along the winding narrow path. At the lichen-encrusted seat, you might like a pause to enjoy the fabulous view of Ullswater. It was along the shore below that William and Dorothy Wordsworth were enchanted by 'A host, of golden daffodils; Beside the lake, beneath the trees, Fluttering and dancing in the breeze.' Then head on along the path as it gradually descends. To your left is the crenellated Lyulph's Tower (alas not open to the public).

With the tower goes the romantic legend immortalised by William Wordsworth in his poem *The Somnambulist*. The legend tells of a beautiful damsel named Emma who was betrothed to an Arthurian knight, Sir Eglamore. He stayed away so long from his beloved, fighting·evil, that in her distress she took to sleep-walking. When he did return, in the middle of the night, he met fair Emma close to Aira Force.

Aira Force.

He touched her, she awoke and swooned over the edge. Sir Eglamore rescued her but she died in his arms. He became a hermit, living in a cave beside the waterfall.

Where the path divides, take the short grassy left fork, to climb a stile into the environs of Aira Beck. Turn left and descend to your outward route, where you turn left again to return to the car park.

16

Maiden Castle

Length of walk: 3¹/₂ miles
Time: 2 hours
Terrain: Easy walking underfoot.
Start/finish: Dunmallard car park, Pooley Bridge, grid ref 470245
Toilets: In car park
Map: OS Explorer OL 5

A circular walk from Dunmallard Hill, Pooley Bridge, along excellently waymarked paths, through fine woodland, over pastures to the site of Maiden Castle.

Return to the entrance of the car park and take the kissing gate on the right into the trees that cover the entire slopes of Dunmallard Hill. Turn right and ascend the pleasing track. Follow it round within the edge of the fine deciduous wood. When you have almost completed a circuit of the wood you will have arrived within sound and almost sight of the B5320. Here take a narrow path that drops, right, to a stile over the boundary fence of the woodland. Walk on a couple of steps to join a good path on the bank above the road, with delightful glimpses through gaps in the hedge of Ullswater and the fells on its opposite shore.

On reaching the A592, cross with care, and walk on a few steps to take a gate in the hedge, on your right. Turn left and follow the hedge to climb the next stile. Head on a short distance to reach a track where you turn right and climb the long fell slope, passing under an isolated group of trees. Continue to the next waymark where you walk left. Stride across the fine pasture, following more markers that lead you easily into Salmond's Plantation. Go on the rising path through ash woodland. Climb the next stile and turn sharp right to climb again to the next waymark, which directs you left and then, almost immediately, left again. Now you are very high above the lake and here the path levels.

Climb the stile at the corner of Rumney's Plantation and walk on beside the conifers to climb the next stile. Ahead are fine views of the Lakeland fells. Follow the path down the slope, coming close to the fence on your right, which encloses a new hedge. Continue to the corner of a mature hedge.

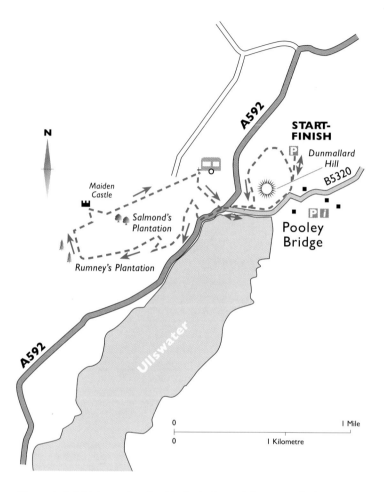

Here, wind right to continue beside the hedge and then a new hedge, to your right. Just before a barn, climb a stile to walk beside it. Go on over the pasture, with the hedge on your left.

At the corner, take the stile on your left to climb steeply up beside a fence on your left to climb another stile to the site of Maiden Castle. This is believed to have been a defended settlement, probably of a family group, who lived close to arable land, about the first millenium BC. You can just make out a ditch, and an outer and an inner rampart. Two small circular areas, just visible, may have been the platforms for circular huts.

Return to cross the stile and then drop diagonally down to a stile in the left corner. Go on to climb the next two stiles, with a pretty tree-lined stream to your left. Keep to the path as it goes on to a stile in the far left corner. This gives access to a narrow road. Cross and walk ahead to pass a ruined farm building and then a gracious house, with caravans close up to its entrance. Walk on a short distance to follow a way-mark directing you right. Where the track turns left, follow the arrow directing you right. Carry on ahead to follow a short track through a hedge to come to the front of the house, where you are directed left.

Ivy-leaved toadflax is a perennial which grows on rocks and walls.

Walk a good track, and descend steps to go through a gate onto a pasture. Descend again to pass through a gate and then on to the gate onto the A592, taken earlier. Turn left, cross the road and take the path along the banking above the road. Go through a gate and stroll the pleasing track through Dunmallard's woodland to arrive at the car park.

Before you leave, cross the lovely arched bridge built over the River Eamont where it emerges from Ullswater to walk through the busy village of Pooley Bridge. Pooley stands for the 'mound or hill by the pool', the hill being the thickly wooded Dunmallard Hill around which you started and ended your walk. On the top of this hill, traces of a pre-Roman fort were found, but today nothing remains and the view from this high point is obscured by conifers

Pooley Bridge and Dacre

Length of walk: 5 miles
Time: 3 hours
Terrain: Easy walking. Short, steepish climb at the start.
Two very brief stretches of the A592 cannot be avoided.
Start/finish: Dunmallard car park, grid ref 469245, on the west
side of the River Eamont at Pooley Bridge.
Toilets: Cross the bridge and walk left through the village.
Map: OS Explorer OL5

A circular walk from Pooley Bridge over pastures on clear paths and tracks to delightful Dacre Church, dramatic Dacre Castle and gracious Dalemain, returning beside the surging River Eamont.

Walk to the entrance of the car park on the B5320 and take the kissing gate on the right to follow the track leading right, signposted 'Dacre'. Climb the wide way below an arch of trees. At the three-armed signpost, leave the woodland and pass through an easy-to-miss gate on the right. Stride across the pasture to climb a stile and continue in the same general direction to the next stile. Beyond, turn left as directed by an arrow and descend by the wall to a stile to the A592, which you cross with care.

Go through the kissing-gate opposite and walk ahead, following the signposted way (directions on pieces of slate). Climb the slope to a stepped stile over a wall into a very narrow lane. Turn right and walk to the T-junction, where you turn left. Use the wide green verge to walk towards Dacre. Cross the single arched bridge over the beck and stroll on to the centre of the village. Then take a right turn and walk up the little hill to St Andrew's. Go inside the lovely church, parts of which date from Norman times. Outside in the churchyard are four carved

A Dacre 'bear'.

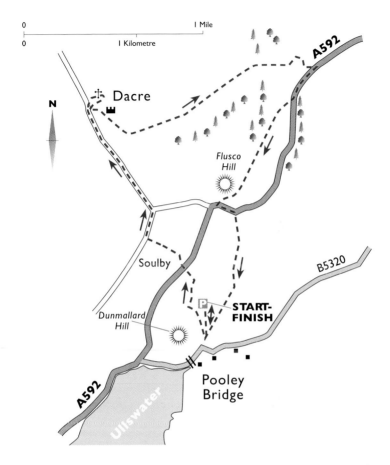

bears which sit near the corners of the church. Nikolaus Pevsner suggests in his *The Buildings of England* series that these bears might mark the four corners of an ancient churchyard.

Leave by the gate in the south wall, bear right and follow the track round left to dramatic Dacre Castle, a fourteenth-century pele tower, with walls seven feet thick. It provided protection for the villagers and their stock against marauders from over the border. It is not open to the public.

Continue along the cart track, with the castle to your right. The way passes beside large pastures, shadowed by a row of poplars, to the outbuildings of

21

Dalemain, a fine country house. Look left over a gate as you go, from where you can often see a herd of fallow deer. Follow the track as it bears round right into a large cobbled courtyard. The house and gardens are open to the public and in the courtyard is a board detailing the cost of entry. There is also a gift shop, restaurant and two museums.

Follow the track, by the courtyard on your right. Continue towards the A592, along a track that swings sharp left. Beyond the gate, turn right, and using the grass verge walk with care along the A-road, where you have a good view of the Georgian façade to the house. Cross the road bridge over Dacre Beck and take the signposted footpath on the right.

Continue uphill on a faint path, over pasture — where in March you might spot hares 'boxing' — to come to the side of a wood. Where the track veers

Bog asphodel has distinctive spiky yellow flowers.

off to the right, go ahead to the waymarked stile. Keep to the left of the fence and go on to the next stile, with fine views ahead. Climb the stile at the foot of the hill and walk ahead to a sturdy sandstone stile, which gives access to the A-road again.

Cross and walk left, using the verge until you reach a signposted stile on the right. Cross several plank bridges. Keep beside the field edge on your left, to take a stile on the left at the end of another magnificent row of poplars. Walk on a narrow path, beside a large pool, to a kissing-gate. Amble on along the distinct path through lovely meadows, coming close to the River Eamont. A final kissing-gate gives access to the woodland at the foot of Dunmallard Hill. Follow the track to return to the parking area and the village.

Barton and Askham Fell

Length of walk: 5¹/₂ miles
Time: 3 hours
Terrain: Suitable for all the family
Start/finish: Car park on the east side of the River Eamont,
Pooley Bridge, grid ref 471244
Toilets: In village
Map: OS Explorer OL5

A circular walk from Pooley Bridge, over pastures to charming St Michael's Church, Barton, returning over Askham Fell.

From the car park, cross the road and turn right along the main street. Pass the information centre and the toilets on your left. Once past the Sun Hotel, turn left to stride beside its wall to go through a gate onto a signposted track. Follow it as it bears right over several stiles, and then through a gate into an area of newly planted trees. At the end of the path, go through a gate and up the slope to take a gate on the left. Stride past Hole House Farm, and then trend slightly right and then left, to go ahead on the signed way, with outbuildings to your right.

Leave by a stile, cross the pasture and climb the next one. In a few steps take the kissing-gate, on the right, into a hedged green lane, and walk left where each hawthorn bush seems full of small birds. At the end of the lane go ahead to a signpost, well left of a ladder-stile (which you ignore). Turn left, go through two gates, on either side of a small stream and follow the continuing track. At the signpost, turn right and stride the track to Barton Church Farm. Barton is not a village; the name refers to buildings belonging to an arable farm.

Follow the track as it winds right to reach the lychgate to the fine Barton Church, which is well worth a visit. It is part-Norman and was built about 1150. The south aisle was added 100 years later because it was too small to house all its worshippers.

The church is a large grey stone building with a squat twelfth-century tower, set centrally and with five-foot-thick walls. Inside, beneath the tower is a

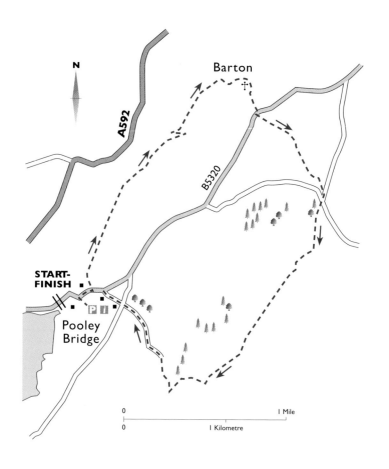

large square area, tunnel-like, supported by two amazing arches. There is much to see, including commemorative wall tablets to members of the Wordsworth family. The church is beautifully situated, with rolling hills all around. Its churchyard is a mass of snowdrops early in the year.

Leave by the lychgate and go on along the access road to join the B5320. Cross and walk right to take the signposted stone step-stile, on your left. Walk ahead over two pastures, with the hedge to your left. Then climb a third field to a stile over a fence, seen clearly up the slope ahead. Continue uphill towards another fence, aiming for the waymarked left corner. Stride on beside the fence and hedge on your right to join a narrow road.

24

The curlew breeds on grassland and moors.

Turn right and walk a few yards to the side of the B-road to Askham. Cross to go through a gate and then an awkward stile into a pasture. Walk ahead, with a copse to your right, to climb a ladder-stile onto a track. Turn right and walk on to pass Winder Hall Farm on your left.

Press on along the continuing track, go through a gate and then head straight up a slope onto moorland. Carry on for half a mile until you reach a wide grassy swathe. Turn right and descend gently for a quarter of a mile to take a narrower grassy path, right, continuing over the moorland towards a wall.

As you near the wall, turn left to head for a row of tall well spaced sycamore and ash trees, just before a wall heading, right, down a slope. At the wall corner wind right and then take another wide grassy swathe, descending quite steeply, keeping parallel with the wall, which now encloses conifers. From this path you have a breathtaking view of Ullswater and the surrounding mountains.

At the bottom of the steep wide grassy track, turn right to walk a stony track to a gate. Beyond join a metalled road and walk on to pass Roehead to your right. Press on down the lane, cross the road that runs along the back of the lake and continue on to wind left through the main street of Pooley Bridge.

Steel Knotts & Pikeawassa

Length: 4 miles
Time: 2-3 hours walking. Thirty-five minutes each way on the Ullswater Steamer.
Terrain: There is a path all the way, two very short stretches of which come close to the edge of the cliff. Children should be under close control on these.
Start/finish: Park at Glenridding pier, grid ref 389170. From here, the ferry takes you to the Howtown pier, on the eastern side of Ullswater. For those who prefer not to take the ferry, the quarry parking at St Peter's Church, Martindale, is at grid ref 436192.
Toilets: Pier at Glenridding and on the boat. None on the walk.
Map: OS Explorer 5

A circular walk from Howtown, which ascends Steel End, then in a series of small steady climbs, Steel Knotts and the spiky summit of Pikeawassa. A long easy descent into Martindale is followed by a pleasing footpath back to the pier. This walk assumes you will want to use the Ullswater ferry (for ferry times, telephone 017684 82229), which is a delight, but plan your day carefully because, if you miss the last ferry, you will have a seven-mile walk back to Glenridding. If you do not wish to take the ferry, use the quarry parking opposite St Peter's Church, Martindale. To reach it, take the long narrow road, from Pooley Bridge, that runs along the south-eastern shore of Ullswater. The quarry lies on the right above the hairpin bends in the road.

Leave Howtown pier and walk ahead to a narrow road. Turn right and, after fifty yards, take a grassy hedged track on the left. Follow it as it winds, right, over the beck and then go on into the tiny hamlet of Howtown. At the T-junction, bear left and walk towards the open fell. Cross the cattle grid and turn right, off the road, to walk beside the fell wall. A short distance along, look for a small manhole cover, with '8 AV 5' inscribed on it, in the centre of the path. To its left is a stone marker.

From immediately behind the marker, ascend the bank that edges the path and go on an indistinct path climbing through bracken to reach a grassy area. Bear steadily half-right, keeping right of some rocks and passing through a

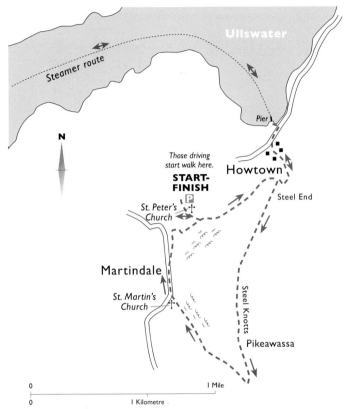

Ullswater

Steamer route

N

Pier

Those driving
start walk here.
**START-
FINISH**

Howtown

St. Peter's
Church

Steel End

Martindale

St. Martin's
Church

Steel Knots

Pikeawassa

0   1 Mile

0   1 Kilometre

short steepish gully. Then the much clearer narrow path continues, the way 'stepped' by other walkers, making it easier to ascend and follow. The route soon becomes clearer and is never in doubt. As it arrives at each little brow, on the way up, that brow always seems the last one until, after three-quarters of a mile, you reach the ridge.

From here you can see the summit, Pikeawassa, standing up proud across the pleasing grassy ridge, encouraging you to hurry on to the 1,414-foot top. But first pause at this end of the ridge, to enjoy the spectacular view into the depths of lovely Martindale and smaller Fusedale, and look back for a grand view of Ullswater.

Then stroll on (you could almost dance) along the fine ridge, with the view improving all the time, to the fine rocks on the summit, Pikeawassa. This may be the place to have your picnic. Then go on ahead to descend the long, easy, narrow path over the short-cropped turf and continue to a sturdy wall. Climb the not very obvious step-stile over it, and walk on along the clear path to where it divides. Here make an acute turn right and walk back to the wall on a lower grassy trod to pass through a gate.

Carry on down the long path, mainly through bracken, for half a mile, to reach the road at Martindale. If you wish to visit St Martin's old church, turn left.

A church has stood on this site for more than 700 years. The flagged floor was laid in the eighteenth century. In 1882 the roof fell in. On that day, in what local people regarded as a miracle, all the parishioners of the valleys were attending the consecration of St Peter's as the new parish church (up the hill and opposite the quarry where you may have parked). In the churchyard of St Martin's is a magnificent

St Martin's Church, Martindale.

yew, where the men of Martindale, famous for their bowmanship, replenished their arms.

Then return to the road and walk right. Less than a quarter of a mile along, take the gate on the right. Beyond, stroll on the grassy way. Continue on to wind round, right, in front of two cottages. Cross their access track and climb up the slope to walk left beside the wall, now on your right. Follow the wall round to go through a gate to walk on to the edge of a small shallow tarn.

Those parking at the quarry should cross the road and walk ahead up a wide track beside St Peter's. Then turn left before the little tarn to join this path. All should walk ahead along the grassy way, below the forbidding side of Steel End, and follow the track as it winds right to come to the manhole cover, with '8 AV 5' inscribed on it. Those who arrived by car turn right here to start their climb to Pikeawassa. Those who arrived by ferry and have nearly completed their walk should continue on to the cattle grid crossed at the outset of the walk. Then turn left and return to the pier.

Hallin Fell

Length of walk: 4 miles
Time: 2-3 hours
**Terrain: Lakeside path, rough in parts. Steepish climb through
woodland. Ascent and descent of the fell on wide grassy swathes.**
**Start/finish: Park at Glenridding pier for Ullswater Steamers to
Howtown Pier. See previous walk for parking at Glenridding pier
or by St Peter's Church, Martindale, if you arrive by car.**
Toilets: At Glenridding, pier head and on boat. None on walk.
Map: OS Explorer 5

*A circular walk from Howtown Pier, along good tracks, through ancient
woodland, over open fell and then onto a fine summit, with superb views up
and down Ullswater and to the Pennines. Ullswater Steamers now run a
winter service. On a fine winter's day, get the first ferry to Howtown, which
gives masses of time to complete your walk at leisure.*

A few steps beyond Howtown jetty, bear right to cross a footbridge and
continue along the edge of the lake. Pass through gates and go on ahead to
go through the kissing gate on the left. Carry on along the pleasing fenced
path to climb steps to a kissing-gate at the top.

Beyond, turn right and follow the glorious path below the steep flanks of
Hallin Fell, with fine views of Ullswater over the wall. Go through a gate
into Hallinhag Wood to stroll the undulating path through the fine oaks of
this ancient woodland, the haunt of woodpecker and jay, and all the tits.

Just before the gate towards the end of the trees, look for an easy-to-miss
narrower path, left, climbing up through the trees, keeping parallel with the
wall to your right. Take your time as you climb and pause regularly to listen
to the birdsong in this pleasing deciduous woodland. Leave the trees by a
kissing gate to walk on a narrow path, beside the continuing wall, on your right.
Follow it as it takes you along the high-level way along the slopes of the fell.

Pause often to look over the wall for one of the magical views of the Lake
District. Below lies Beda Fell, separating Boredale from Martindale. Look
for Steel Knotts *(walk 8)* which hides delightful Fusedale. Beyond, to your

29

left, rears Loadpot Hill, which leads on, eventually, to High Street. To your right stands the huge bulk of Place Fell.

Continue on the glorious path beside the wall until you can look down, steeply, to St Peter's Church. (If you have parked in the quarry opposite the church instead of taking the boat, you start your walk here. In that case, climb up the wide swathe of grass just above the quarry.) Here, where the wall turns down sharply, walkers coming from the ferry turn sharp left and those from the quarry continue upwards. The way is

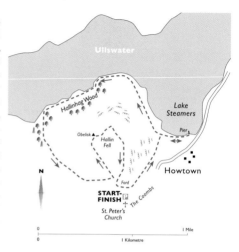

never in doubt. Towards the top of Hallin Fell, the path bears slightly right and brings you to a fine twelve-foot-high obelisk, constructed of square stones. The view is stunning. The summit is mainly grassy but bracken does encroach. There are delightful hollows, in the sun and out of the wind, just right for your picnic.

Leave the north-eastern corner of the summit, on a narrower but equally clear descending grassy trod. At a T-junction, bear left to a cairn, and then follow the grassy swathe as it winds round right and descends steadily to a wide plateau. Here take any of the grassy paths, heading right, south, to arrive back at the wall corner (and a view of St Peter's) and descend a little.

Then bear left along another grassy path, which leads to a water tank. Go behind this and carry on the pleasant path as it continues high above the road and its notorious zigzags. Eventually the path takes you down towards the road and then rises gradually to go on as a delightful terrace-like way, finally to descend to the gate at the top of the steps, taken earlier.

Walkers who have come from the car park should continue on, following the instructions from the second paragraph at the start of the text. Walkers for the ferry should go through the gate and descend the steps to retrace their route to the jetty. Make sure you've timed your walk well, in time to catch your ferry.

Silver Bay

Length of walk: 5 miles
Time: 3 hours
Terrain: Suitable for all the family
Start/finish: Patterdale car park, grid ref 396159

A circular walk from Patterdale car park, on distinct paths and tracks, along the side of Ullswater to Silver Crag. The return is along a higher path, below Place Fell, to continue part way up the path to Boredale Hause. This is followed by a descent to a wide track, which returns you to Patterdale past Crookabeck, with its fascinating angora goats.

The village of Patterdale, which lies at the head of Ullswater, was probably once named St Patrick's Dale. Legend has it that, after being shipwrecked on Duddon Sands, the saint made his way, on foot, to the beautiful dale and baptised the local inhabitants. John Mounsey, 'King of Patterdale', lived at Patterdale Hall. His main claim to fame was that he led a party of dalesmen to Stybarrow Crag *(see walk 3)* when Scottish marauders were expected. He 'stationed' his troops and then left them, saying that he was too lame to fight. Even so, Patterdale won the day.

To start this pleasing walk, turn right out of the car park and walk on to reach the George Starkey Memorial Hut, where you take the signposted right turn just beyond it. Go on the good track to cross Goldrill Beck, which pours its water into the lake, and continue to Side Farm. Pass between the buildings and turn left to walk along a wide track in the direction of the lake. To your right towers Place Fell. Pass below fine trees and then descend a long pitched path, with ever-increasing views of the lake. After a little climb, wind round Silver Crag and walk on to a seat to enjoy the fine view of Silver Bay, the lake and its islands. There is a little sandy bay on the shore, ideal for quiet snoozes and a picnic.

A few steps before the seat, on the right, a steepish stony path ascends a gully, and this you climb. Near the top, pass a little pool on the left and lofty Silver Crag on your right. Ignore the path that drops down to the path taken earlier and stroll the delightful high-level grassy way, enjoying the views ahead and across the valley. Cross several streams and go past two caves, with serious drops in them, almost hidden from view by trees.

31

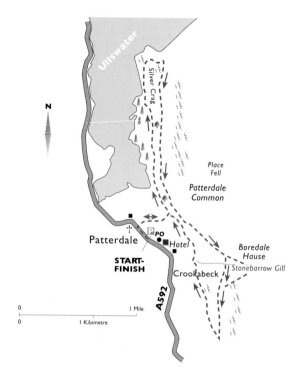

Follow the path through a defunct quarry and carry on above the houses at Rooking. At a choice of paths, take the lower track and walk on, soon to begin a steady climb up the open slopes. After a quarter of a mile, look for a narrow grassy path going off right. This leads to Stonebarrow Gill, which you cross, and then continues on to climb a little onto a wider rougher track.

Turn right and descend for just over half a mile to join a wide track along the valley. Here, turn sharp right to follow the lovely way for just over another half mile. As you near the picturesque Crookabeck, look for the steps, on the right, which lead to a permissive path to take you round behind the dwellings and outbuildings. A stile gives access to the main track once more. Here you might see the dainty angora goats from which mohair is produced. Continue, right, to join the metalled lane at Rooking. Turn right and continue to go through a gate in the direction of Side Farm. Walk the track, a little above the valley pastures on your left, and, at the farm, turn left to pass through the buildings. Head on along the track, cross the beck and, at the main road, turn left for the car park.